SPYROS HOREMIS

VISUAL ILLUSIONS

COLORING BOOK

DOVER PUBLICATIONS, INC., NEW YORK

PUBLISHER'S NOTE

The visual illusions in this book are geometrical line drawings that take cunning advantage of the nature and habits of our eyes, and persuade them to accept an unreal situation.

In most of the examples, mere lines on the flat surface of the sheet conjure up a strong conviction of three-dimensionality. But of a very odd type: as you stare at these drawings, "top" and "bottom" and "in" and "out" change places capriciously. And often the solid object suggested by the linear interplay could not possibly exist even in *three* dimensions.

The coloring of such drawings presents special challenges. First, there is no limitation to your choice of colors. Second, you have the opportunity to enhance the illusion greatly by a careful selection and distribution of the colors. The four examples on the covers, colored by the artist himself, will give you a good idea of what can be achieved.

Published in Canada by General Publishing Company, Ltd.,
30 Lesmill Road, Don Mills, Toronto, Ontario.
Published in the United Kingdom by Constable and Company, Ltd.

Visual Illusions Coloring Book is a new work, first published by Dover Publications, Inc., in 1973.

DOVER *Pictorial Archive* SERIES

This book belongs to the Dover Pictorial Archive Series. You may use the designs and illustrations for graphics and crafts applications, free and without special permission, provided that you include no more than four in the same publication or project. (For permission for additional use, please write to Dover Publications, Inc., 31 East 2nd Street, Mineola, N.Y. 11501.)
However, republication or reproduction of any illustration by any other graphic service whether it be a book or in any other design resource is strictly prohibited.

International Standard Book Number: 0-486-21595-4

MANUFACTURED IN THE UNITED STATES OF AMERICA
Dover Publications, Inc.
31 East 2nd Street
Mineola, N.Y. 11501

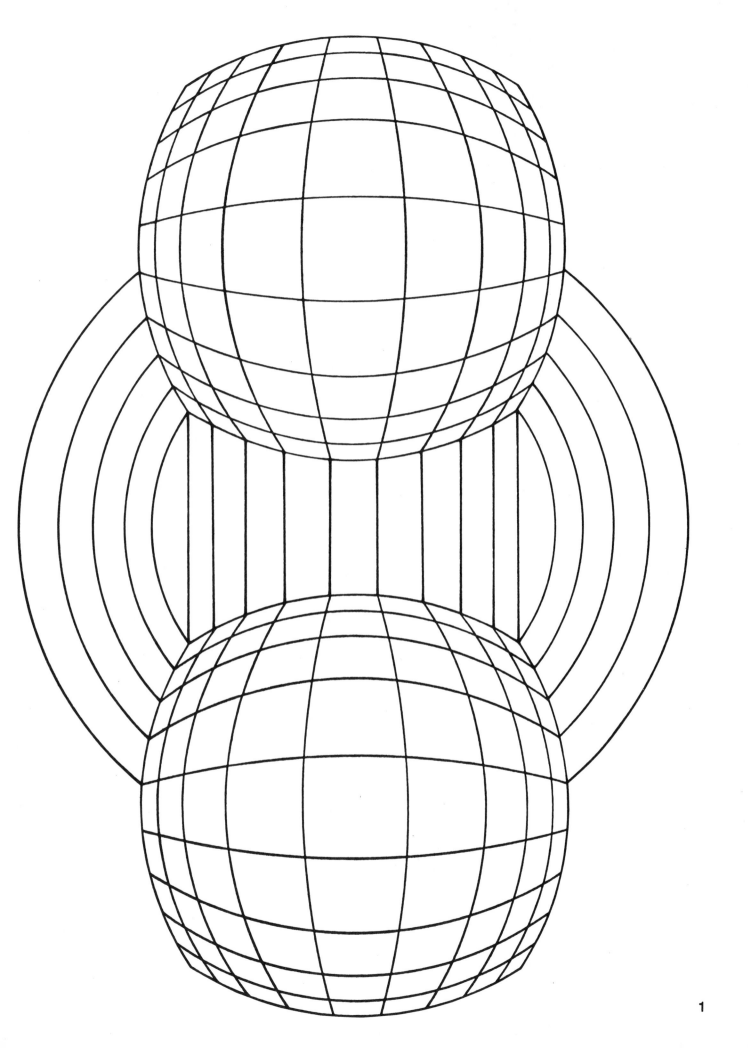

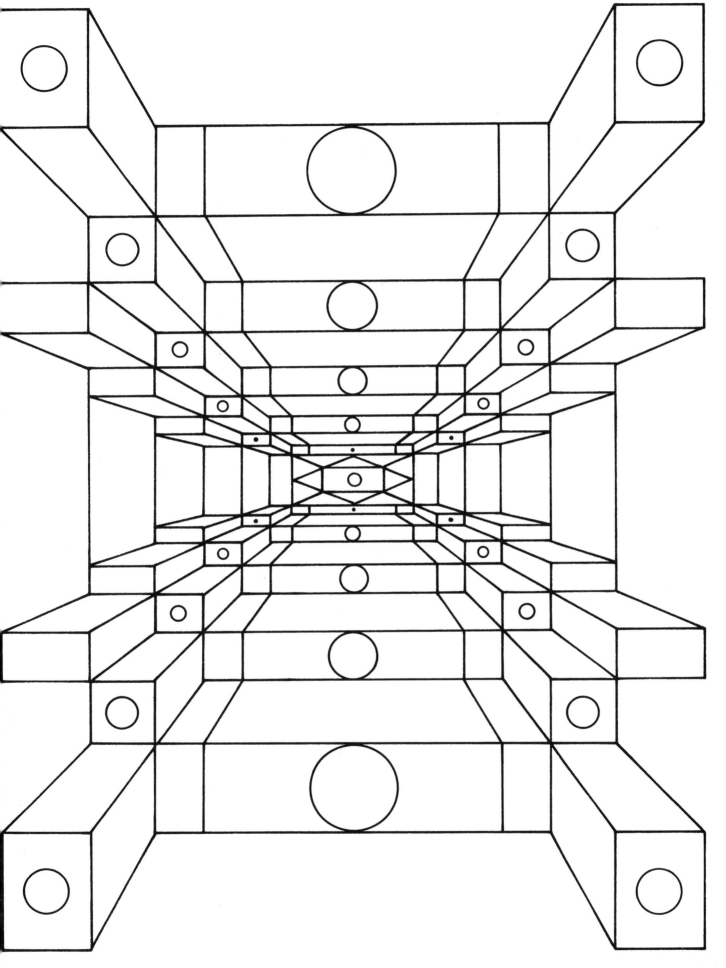

3

4

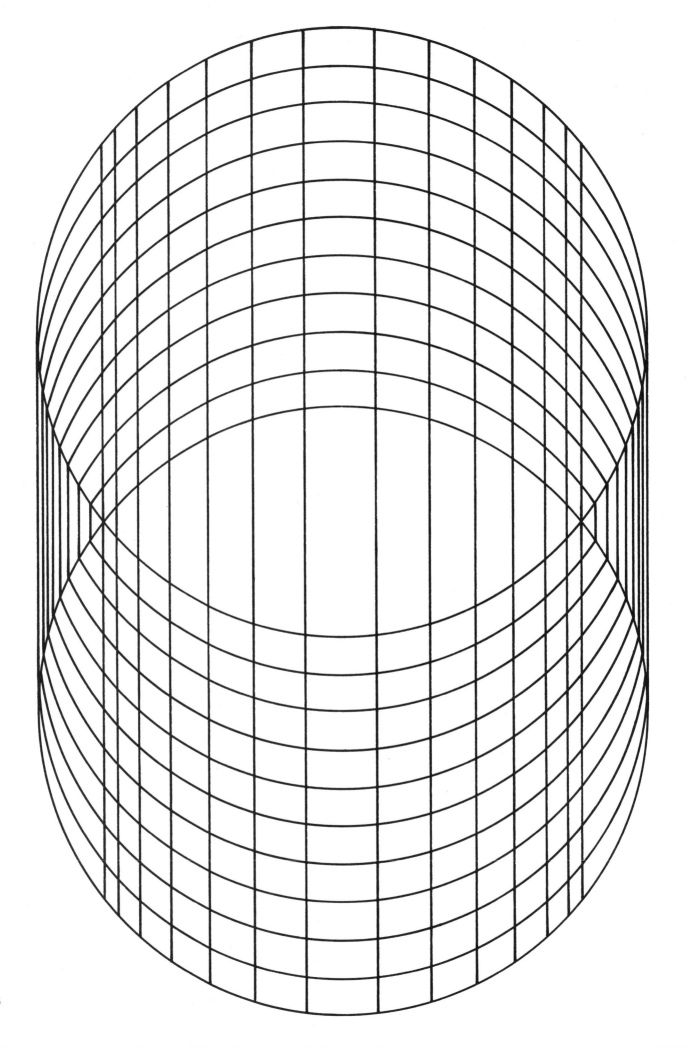

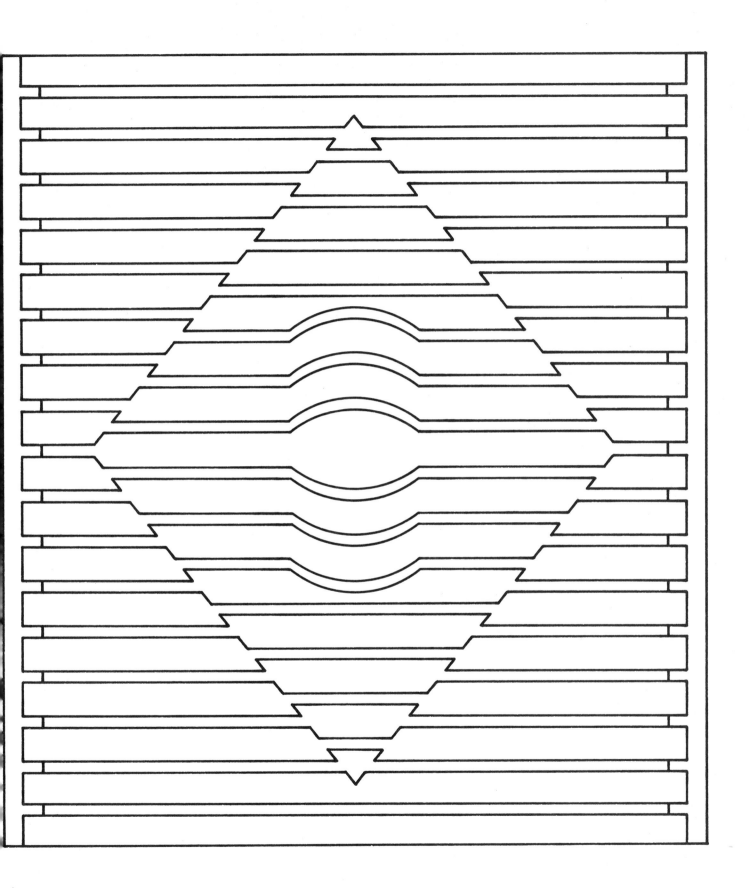

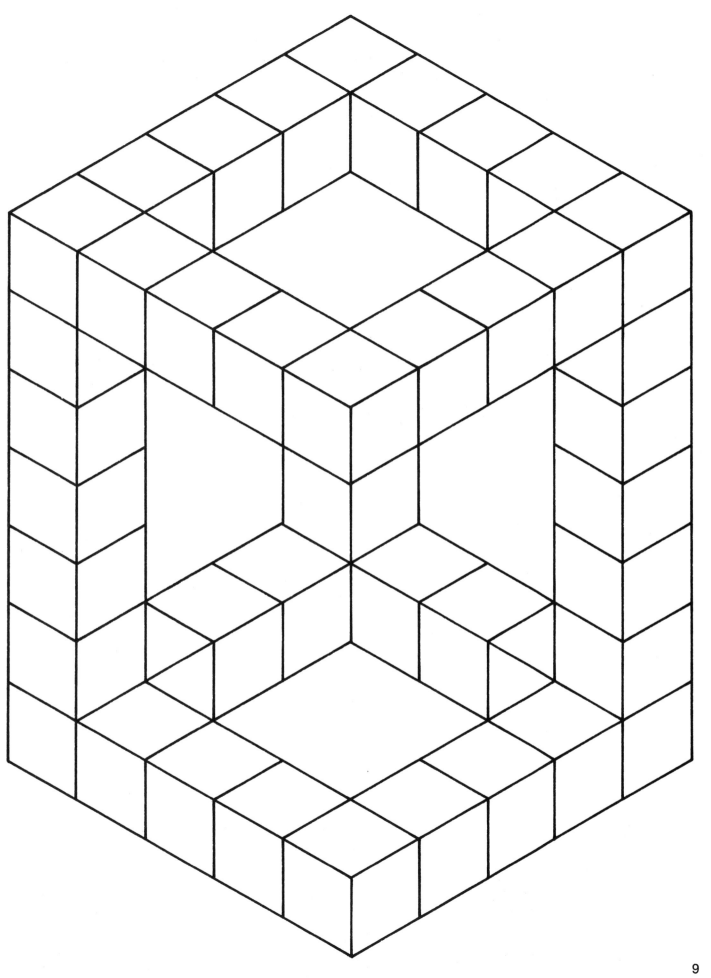

12

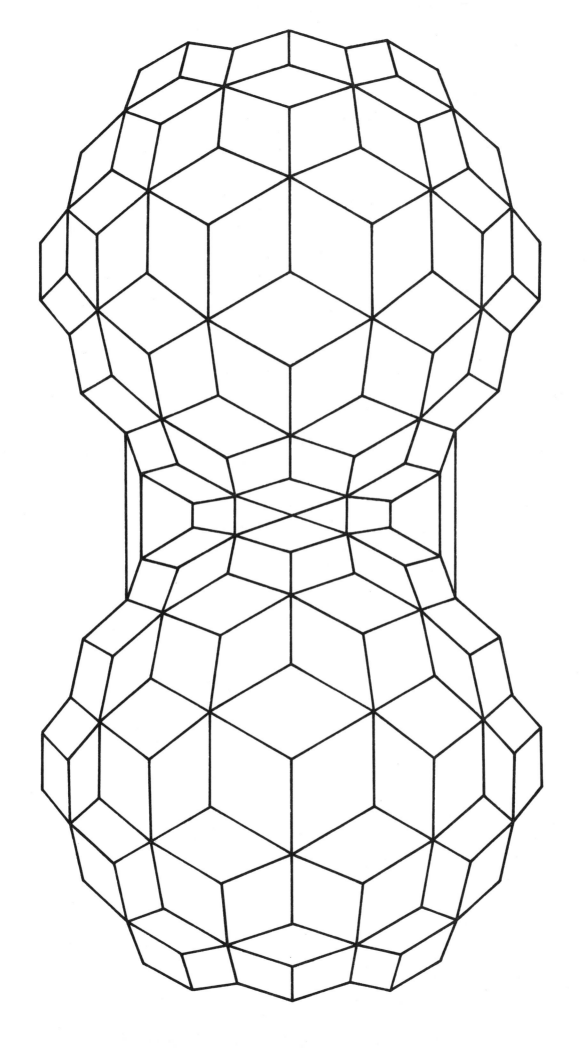

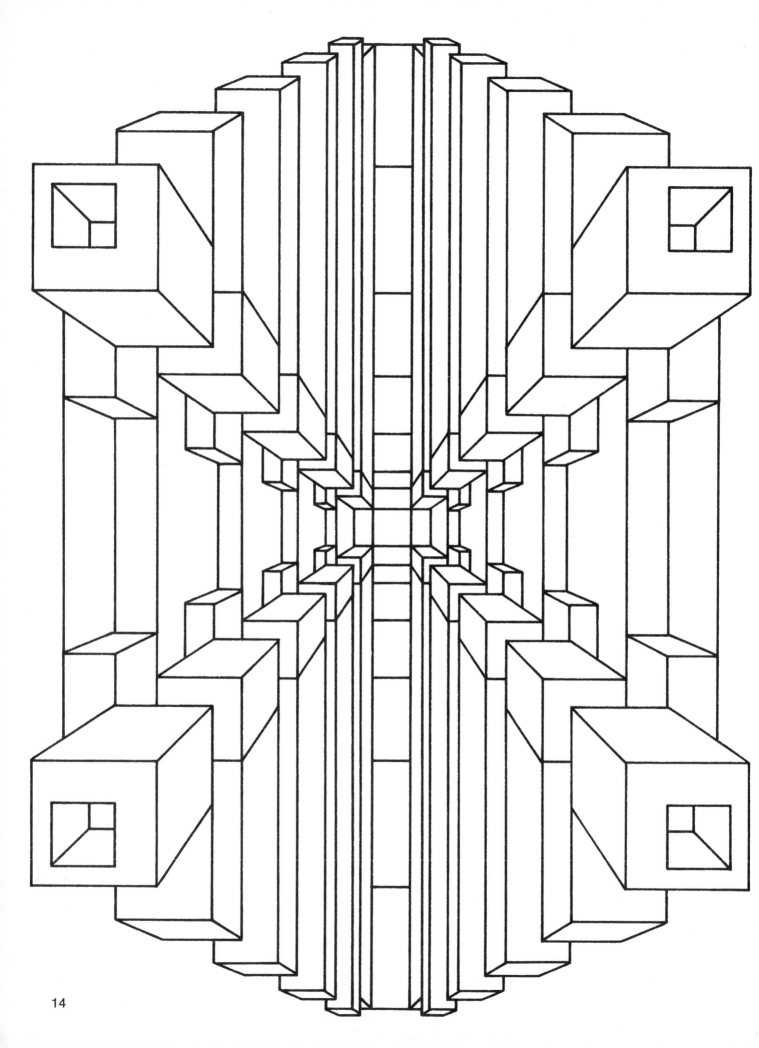

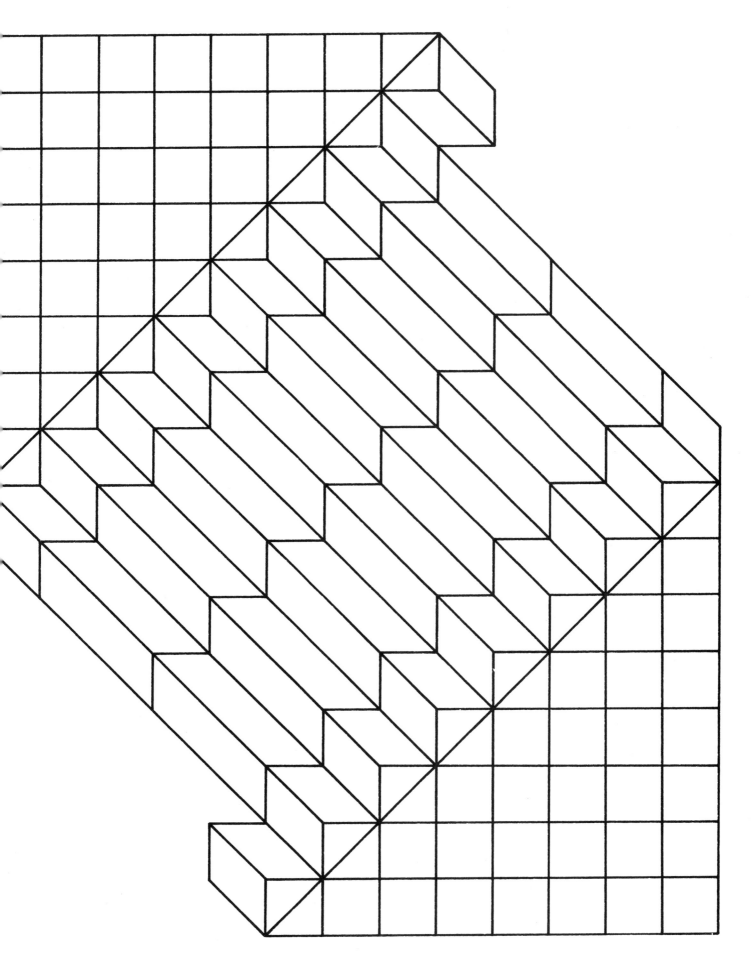

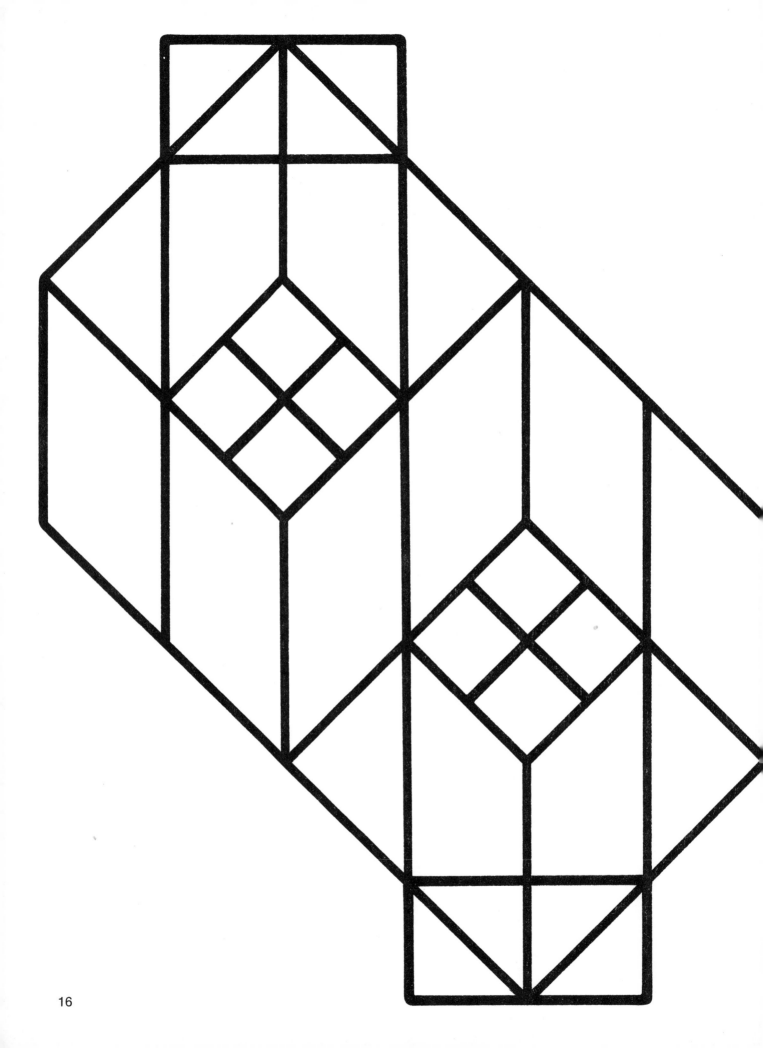

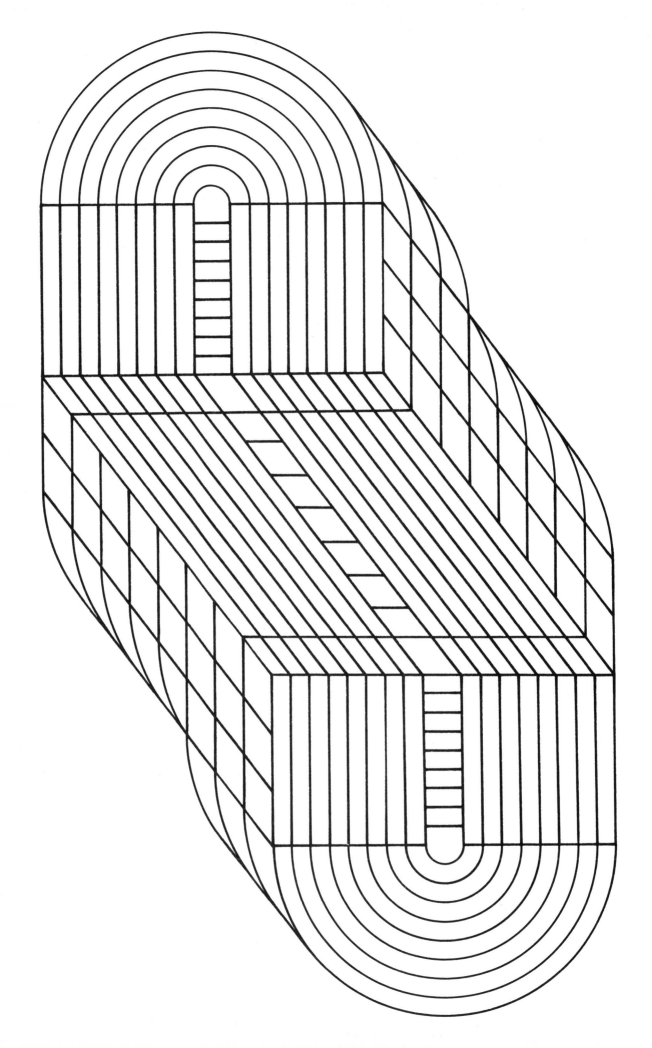

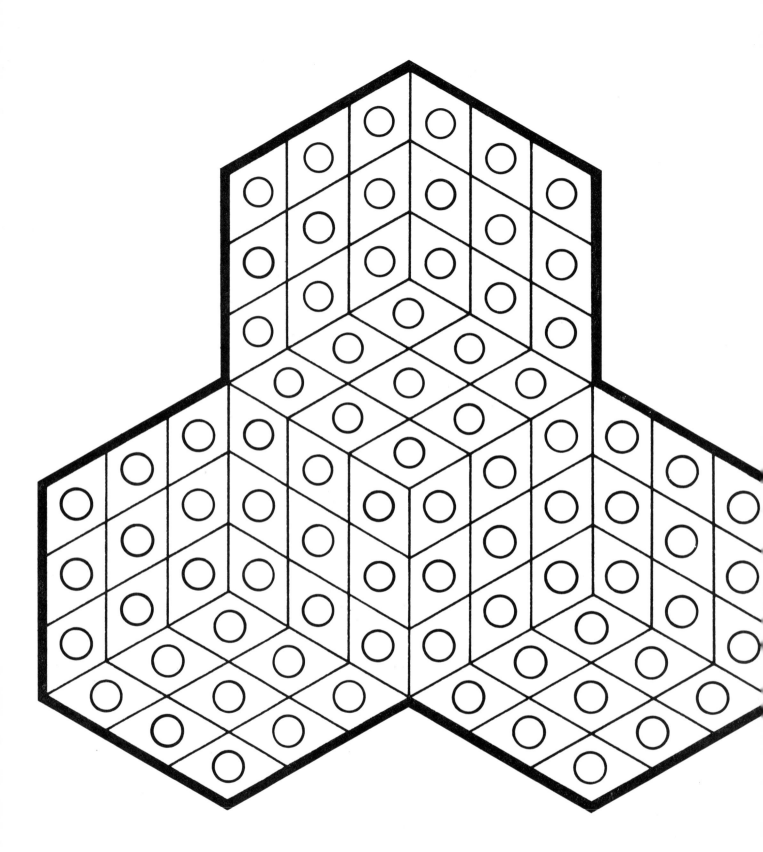

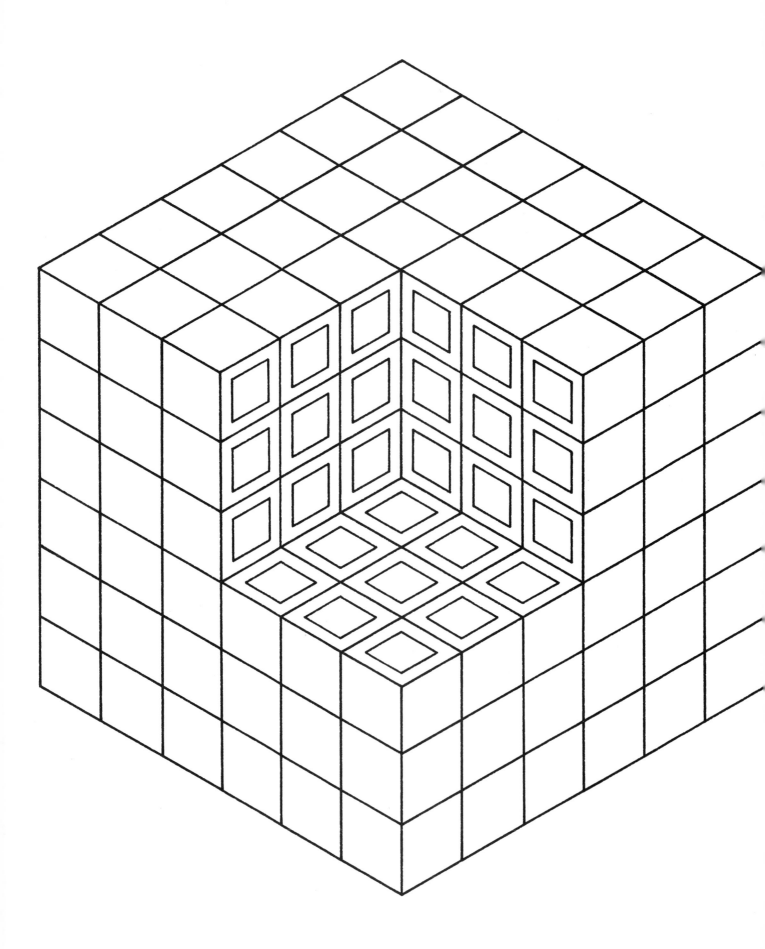

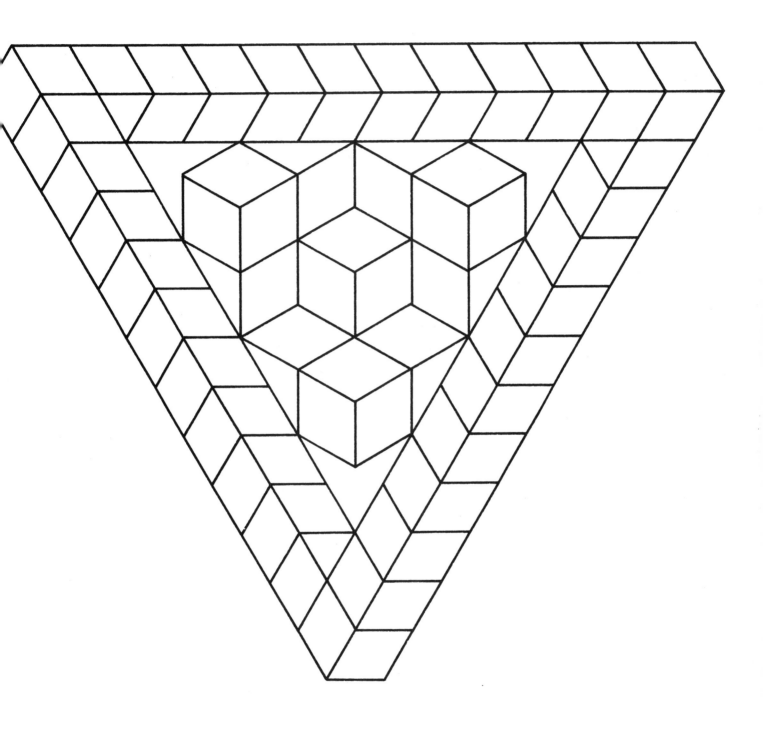

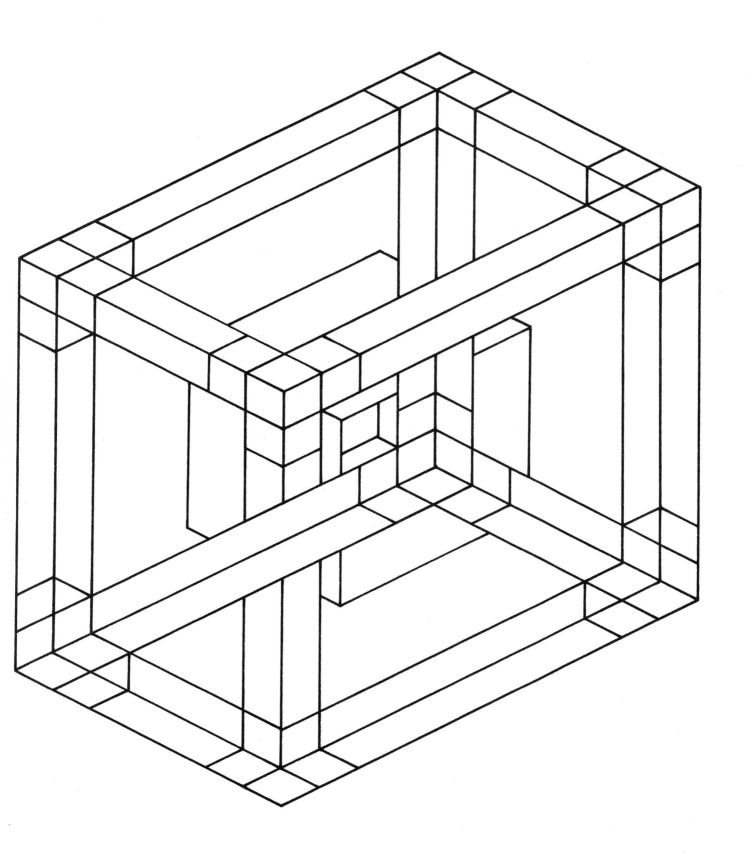